Heal the Land: A Blueprint for Spiritual Restoration

Heal the Land: A Blueprint for Spiritual Restoration

By Stephen E. Boyd, M. Ed.

Copyright

Copyright © 2022 Stephen E. Boyd, M. Ed., Owner, SB Entertainment, LLC, all rights reserved.

Published by PurposeHouse Publishing, Columbia, Maryland.
Cover Design by PurposeHouse Publishing.
Printed in the USA.

No part of this publication may be reproduced or distributed in any form or by any means or stored in a database or retrieval system without the prior written permission of the author.

ISBN: 978-1-957190-07-5

Scripture quotations marked "KJV" are taken from the Holy Bible, King James Version (Public Domain).

Scripture taken from the New King James Version®. Copyright © 1982 by Thomas Nelson. Used by permission. All rights reserved.

Scriptures from the NET Bible® https://netbible.com copyright ©1996, 2019 used with permission from Biblical Studies Press, L.L.C. All rights reserved.

Contents

Introduction 1

Chapter 1: Why Are You Complaining When You Got What You Wanted? 5

Chapter 2: Commitment: Process Before Product 19

Chapter 3: Healing the Land: A Blueprint to Spiritual Restoration 35

Introduction

In high school, I had a teacher for Algebra I and II who was a very 'spirited' teacher. He talked with a funny, groggy voice and was quite animated while teaching. I loved how he dramatized word problems, making funny noises, contorting his body, and engaging the class to mimic his actions! The unfortunate thing for me was I did not learn anything!

Mathematicians know that math is all about operations, systems, and functions. As you progress in math, the more you know and understand those systems, the better you can handle more complex problems. I must have missed something somewhere because math knowledge did not make me an ideal math student. One specific realm of expertise I needed to be successful was understanding the order of operations. The order of operations is a system of dissecting formulas. It wasn't until I was an adult that I learned an acronym I was never taught; had I known this, I would have been much more successful. The acronym is: Please, Excuse, My, Dear, Aunt, Sally. This acronym stands for Parenthesis, Exponents, Multiplication, Division, Addition, and Subtraction. In other words, no matter how complex the formula is, if the student followed the order of operations, one could successfully solve the problem—getting the correct answer. Unfortunately for me, I did not know the formula. So I struggled because I was never given the formula.

We are living in times of desperation, a tipping point in our world where the inward envy and jealousy in the hearts of men are bringing us to utter collapse! Additionally, the rise of natural disasters like hurricanes, Tsunamis, earthquakes, and volcanic eruptions leaves people desperately asking, "Where is God in all this mayhem?" The Bible says in Romans 8:20-22 NET says:

> For the creation was subjected to futility-not willingly but because God who subjected it-in hope that the creation itself will also be set free from the bondage of decay into the

glorious freedom of God's children. For we know that the whole creation groans and suffers together until now.

In fact, Jesus said in Matthew 24:5-8 NET:

For many will come in my name, saying, 'I am the Christ,' and they will mislead many. You will hear of wars and rumors of wars. Make sure that you are not alarmed, for this must happen, but the end is still to come. For nation will rise up in arms against nation, and kingdom against kingdom. And there will be famines and earthquakes in various places. All these things are the beginning of birth pains.

While these things reflect our current state, ultimately, it is because we are not adhering to a fundamental formula God has given us to bring order and restoration to the world. This formula is found in 2 Chronicles 7:14. God told Solomon, "If my people, which are called by my name, shall humble themselves, and pray, and seek my face, and turn from their wicked ways; then will I hear from heaven, and will forgive their sin, and heal their land."

This book is dedicated to helping you 'dissect' God's formula towards spiritual restoration, renewal, revival, and reconciliation. While I'd like to believe that no one has to tell us, we are in the middle of proverbial shark-infested waters, with blood in the water. But given how bland and unassuming people are living these days, I'm here to announce that this world is in the middle of shark-infested waters and blood all around us—and we are the bait!

God has impressed upon me to write this book to 'throw out the lifeline' and call God's creation back to order and righteousness with him. When we realign our focus on God's priorities, we will see hope restored to a dying world. There is a revival coming! First, however, we must adhere to the formula.

Advancing the Kingdom,
Stephen E. Boyd

Chapter 1

Why Are You Complaining When You Got What You Wanted?

You waited all week long for the weekend. Finally, it's Friday. Yes! It's time to relax and enjoy good friends and food at your favorite restaurant. After a short wait, your restaurant pager goes off, and it's time to be seated at your table. As you follow the waiter down the aisle, you notice someone else's order and ask the waiter, "What's that they're eating? It looks good!" The waiter replies and explains the dish. It looks so good, and after hearing the waiter's response, it sounds good too. So, you forcefully tell the waiter, "I'll have what they're having."

After placing your order, you have great expectations while waiting for your food to come out. You smile as your food arrives and take the highly anticipated first bite. But, to your surprise, what looked so good and sounded so good doesn't taste good. In anger and disappointment, you call the waiter back to your table. You got what you asked for but discovered that it didn't satisfy you and must be changed. What a great lesson to learn—the things others have can look good and sound good, but that doesn't mean they are best for us.

Israel learned this lesson when they asked God to give them a king. They were disappointed with their state of affairs, looked at other nations with kings, and wanted to be like them. They thought the proverbial "grass was greener" in the other nations, and through comparison, they became discontent with having God as their king. They wanted a human being they could hail. Their invisible King of all Kings who had brought them out of the bondage of Egypt was no longer enough—they wanted to be like other nations. The passage in 1 Samuel 8 describes the situation.

> Then all the elders of Israel gathered together and came to Samuel at Ramah, [5] and said to him, "Look, you are old, and your sons do not walk in your ways. Now make us a king to judge us like all the nations." [6] But the thing displeased Samuel when they said,

> "Give us a king to judge us." So Samuel prayed to the LORD. **7** And the LORD said to Samuel, "Heed the voice of the people in all that they say to you; for they have not rejected you, but they have rejected Me, that I should not reign over them. **8** According to all the works which they have done since the day that I brought them up out of Egypt, even to this day—with which they have forsaken Me and served other gods—so they are doing to you also. **9** Now therefore, heed their voice. However, you shall solemnly forewarn them, and show them the behavior of the king who will reign over them." **10** So Samuel told all the words of the LORD to the people who asked him for a king. (1 Samuel 8:4-10 NKJV)

Like a parent who knows something is not good for their child but lets them have it to teach them a lesson, God tells Samuel to heed the voice of the elders and let Israel have their human king. However, God's concession is not without a caveat. He tells the prophet to warn them that what they want may not turn out how they think it will. Their new king may not be as merciful as their heavenly King of all Kings had been. Samuel conveys the warning to the people who had asked for a king. Yet, despite a warning from Almighty God himself, the people still insisted on having an earthly king. That is the danger of covetousness. It blinds you with a belief that you're missing something when, in in fact, you have everything you need.

Covetousness blinds you with a belief that you're missing something when, in in fact, you have everything you need.

Covetousness is an inordinate desire for another's possessions, craving possessions, or wishing earnestly for what belongs to another. Israel was guilty of this ancient sin, and God said they had not rejected Saul. They had rejected him from reigning over them. Sadly, they had no idea what they were requesting. Like someone who looks at another person's plate at a restaurant, orders what they are having, and gets disappointed when they taste it, Israel sets herself up for great disappointment. The king they so earnestly desired made horrible decisions and sinned against God. He took the nation into a downward spiral. He kept back the spoil and disobeyed the voice of the Lord to destroy the Amalekites utterly. He even consulted witches under cover of night when he could no longer hear the voice of the Lord. Israel couldn't see their king's pending downfall at the time because the trap of comparison and the danger of covetousness had blinded their eyes. Israel had to learn this valuable lesson: *We are where we are because God gave us what we requested. And now we're mad at God—not the world and not ourselves.*

Israel isn't the only nation that could say the same thing. How many times have we voted for elected officials and been sadly disappointed? They didn't keep their promises, and rather than making things better, things got worse. We can all learn a lesson from Israel, which is the danger of covetousness and unintended consequences.

The Law of Unintended Consequences™

A consequence is often unanticipated. It is the outcome or result that materializes because of a decision or action. It has been described as the effect that results from a cause, the reaction to an action, or the unintentional result of doing something. Covetousness often has unintended consequences because, on the surface getting what we want makes us feel better. It may even temporarily improve our lives but still later be detrimental.

Whenever we covet things that seemingly make life better, we must realize there's always the potential for an unintended consequence. For example, whenever there is a technological innovation, it first appears to make things better. The invention of the remote control for televisions was the ultimate convenience. However, it also facilitates sitting for hours in front of a television without moving. Similarly, the Internet makes information readily accessible but often puts us at our desks, computers, and smart TVs for hours. The same innovation that seemingly makes life better also fosters a sedentary lifestyle and adverse health effects. Other examples include the invention of cars, buses, and trailers. They add convenience to our lives but have environmental consequences.

Perhaps one of the greatest examples of unintended consequences is in relationships. Many single people want to be in a relationship, so they are not the only one who is alone. However, rushing into a relationship, so you are not "the odd one out" without a date means you are not taking time to ask questions and get to know the person. That can lead to serious unintended consequences. They may prove to be unstable, dishonest, abusive, or a possessor of other negative habits that adversely affect your life. In other words, they may have a hidden side that is not worth the initial upside to entering the relationship.

There are indeed unintentional consequences, and they are like the hidden side to the upside. God gave Israel what they asked for and warned them. But they did not take the time to consider the consequences. We must all take the time to consider the magnitude or impact on the backside of what might happen if we get what we want. God explained the consequences to Israel. Here's what he said:

> So Samuel told all the words of the LORD to the people who asked him for a king. [11] And he said, "This will be the behavior of the king who will reign over you: He will take your sons and appoint *them* for his own chariots and *to be* his horsemen, and *some* will run before his chariots. [12] He will appoint captains over his thousands and captains over his fifties, *will set some* to plow his ground and reap his harvest, and *some* to

make his weapons of war and equipment for his chariots. **13** He will take your daughters *to be* perfumers, cooks, and bakers. **14** And he will take the best of your fields, your vineyards, and your olive groves, and give *them* to his servants. **15** He will take a tenth of your grain and your vintage and give it to his officers and servants. **16** And he will take your male servants, your female servants, your finest young men, and your donkeys, and put *them* to his work. **17** He will take a tenth of your sheep. And you will be his servants. **18** And you will cry out in that day because of your king whom you have chosen for yourselves, and the LORD will not hear you in that day." **19** Nevertheless the people refused to obey the voice of Samuel; and they said, "No, but we will have a king over us, **20** that we also may be like all the nations, and that our king may judge us and go out before us and fight our battles." **21** And Samuel heard all the words of the people, and he repeated them in the hearing of the LORD. **22** So the LORD said to Samuel, "Heed their voice, and make them a king." (1 Samuel 8:10-22a NKJV)

The Lord describes a king that would take their sons and daughters as meager servants, eat the best of their fields, and take a tenth of their grain and sheep. He tells them they will cry out in anguish because of this very king they are asking for, but they don't listen. Why? They wanted to be like others. God gave them what they asked for even though he warned them. Notice that they would cry out to him because of the king they wanted. How is it that God warned them, and they still wanted it, but when it went awry, it was God they would go back to and cry about it? We may respond to their actions in disgust but must also realize that we do the same thing in so many ways. We do the same thing when our allegiance to a political party is greater than our allegiance to him and when we ignore his warnings about something and do it anyway.

That is what happens when God gives us something that he knows is not good for us, and he must watch the harm that results because we ignore his warning. That's where we are in our country. We want our moral and immoral freedoms, big cars and technology, LGBT equality, money at the expense of justice, and more. But look at the unintended consequence of us telling God, "How dare you not give me what I want!" Where we are in our country is a result of the things we said we wanted, and God said okay.

> *We are where we are because God gave us what we requested. And now we're mad at God—not the world and not ourselves.*

Like Adam and Eve in the garden, we have so much but want the one thing God warns us not to take. God gave them access to everything in the Garden of Eden. They had all of paradise at their disposal except for one tree he told them not to touch. He instructed them not to eat from that tree, but he did not take away their power of choice. Eve chose to listen to the serpent, and Adam decided to follow his wife. The unintended consequence was sin, spiritual death, and banishment from the place that had been created for them. They were out of place, out of position, and out of intimate fellowship with God. Things were "out of whack."

The chaotic state of the world is a result of the same sin called covetousness. Wealth is unequally distributed, and countries loaded with rich natural resources are in poverty. Many cities and rural areas in the United States are contending with poverty, which leads to violence. The Centers for Disease Control (CDC) reports that the United States murder rate rose 30% between 2019 and 2020—the largest single-year increase in more than a century.[1] Their findings align with FBI numbers.

These things and more are the consequences of our nation's decisions and actions. Our covetousness has brought us to this place. But, with so much going on, one may wonder how and if it can be fixed. Can we cure the unintended consequences?

Doctor, is there a cure?

"A patient cured is a customer lost." – Big Pharma

Like Big Pharma prescribes medicines for what needs to be fixed instead of getting to the root with pre-existing natural cures, our governments often invest money into programs that make a good effort but bring no long-lasting change. Can we afford to continue putting band-aids on matters of the heart? Surely, we can't. And we must also realize that

---

[1] John Gramlich, "What we know about the increase in U.S. murders in 2020," Pew Research Center, October 27, 2021, https://www.pewresearch.org/fact-tank/2021/10/27/what-we-know-about-the-increase-in-u-s-murders-in-2020/

there's no quick fix to what ails our nation. If we will see change, we must commit to a recovery process and a mindset shift.

Like the Israelites who went back to the God who warned them in the first place, we must have a change of mind. We must go back to God for the blueprint needed to bring change to our nation, and we must not go back to him expecting an easy or quick fix. All of us have been in situations where we wanted out, and we wanted out quickly. Still, there are some things we must walk out of via a process. Some things won't be changed overnight. For example, if you have a child with someone—even if you're not married—you must work together over the long haul to parent the child. There are some things you must work through, pray through, and be patient whether you were the culprit or something happened to you over which you had no control.

Lasting change for the better seldom happens overnight. Typically, change requires a process called transition. If you don't go through the process, you don't get the change you want to see. So, the real question isn't whether there's a cure; it's whether we will commit to the process necessary for change.

God revealed the key to long-lasting change to Solomon only after he went through a process.

In the next chapter, we explore the process, and the key steps Solomon went through before God revealed a blueprint for long-lasting change to him. During this process, Solomon showed commitment, humility, and a desire for true wisdom. We can achieve the same results if we commit to the process with humility and a true desire for wisdom. So let's get ready to uncover the wisdom embedded in Solomon's process. Let's discover the cure.

Chapter 2

Commitment: Process Before Product

Change is not an event, it's a process. – Barbara Johnson

Success is a process, not an event. – Gary Halbert

In success, people see only the product. But they do not know the details of the process. - Lailah Gifty Akita

Products fuel life's conveniences. Computers replaced typewriters and made typing easier. Wireless earbuds replaced cordless headphones and made listening easier. Automobiles make daily commutes easier. Yet, we often take these modern conveniences for granted and fail to realize they each began as processes before they were products. They were conceived as ideas that were modeled, prototyped, and tested before they were released to the market.

A process is necessary for change. We know the ills that plague our nation and may want change immediately. However, long-lasting change requires a process. Change is not an event, it's a process, and to see the change we want, we must commit to a process.

Solomon models what it looks like to go through a process before receiving a blueprint, revelation, or strategy for his desired change for his nation. He had a seemingly overwhelming responsibility to follow in his father's, King David's, footsteps. He responded by asking God for wisdom to lead his nation instead of riches or wealth for himself. He then went through a series of processes that empowered him to lead his nation to greatness and receive God's blueprint for national restoration.

If we want to see long-lasting change for our nation, there are some key lessons to learn from Solomon's process. We can glean insight from what he did before he received God's blueprint for national restoration and healing. Solomon demonstrates that to receive a blueprint from God, the process involves:

1. Building a foundation
2. Sanctification
3. Communication
4. Revelation

Let's explore each in more detail.

Building a Foundation

> So all the work that Solomon had done for the house of the LORD was finished; and Solomon brought in the things which his father David had dedicated: the silver and the gold and all the furnishings. And he put *them* in the treasuries of the house of God. **2** Now Solomon assembled the elders of Israel and all the heads of the tribes, the chief fathers of the children of Israel, in Jerusalem, that they might bring the ark of the covenant of the LORD up from the City of David, which *is* Zion. **3** Therefore all the men of Israel assembled with the king at the feast, which *was* in the seventh month. **4** So all the elders of Israel came, and the Levites took up the ark. **5** Then they brought up the ark, the tabernacle of meeting, and all the holy furnishings that *were* in the tabernacle. The

priests and the Levites brought them up. ⁶ Also King Solomon, and all the congregation of Israel who were assembled with him before the ark, were sacrificing sheep and oxen that could not be counted or numbered for multitude. ⁷ Then the priests brought in the ark of the covenant of the LORD to its place, into the inner sanctuary of the temple, to the Most Holy *Place,* under the wings of the cherubim. (2 Chronicles 5:1-7 NKJV)

As the passage from 2 Chronicles 5 indicates, Solomon took over his father's charge to build a temple for God. He brings the ark of the covenant to the Temple and organizes the priests and worshippers for God's glory. He commits to the process of building and finishes the work. The temple was complete and functioning under the Levitical order that God had given his father.

If we follow Solomon's model, we must ask, "What are we building?" Are we building our lives and nation on spiritual principles? For Solomon, building a foundation for his nation wasn't just the physical activity of getting the priests or the physical structure of the Temple in order. He put his spiritual priorities in order by asking for wisdom to build and lead his nation. That was his foundation.

If we want a revelation from God, we must ask whether we have inspected our foundation? Our character? Is our individual and national character in alignment with God's word. Like Solomon organizing the carpenters and mansions for the Temple, are we getting the stones of our lives in order? We are the temple of the Holy Ghost.

Solomon also aligned the priests and Levites. There is physical and spiritual alignment by the time we get to 2 Chronicles chapter six. That all speaks to foundation, order, and structure. What are we doing to get physically in alignment? What are we doing to get spiritually in alignment—individually and as a nation?

Being Christ-like means committing to the disciplines necessary to develop Christ-like character and bring our lives, nation, and national thinking into alignment. Many shirk this discipline by saying, "God knows my heart." But every level at which God would use us requires a higher commitment and mindset. So Solomon lays a foundation, and the next step is sanctification.

Sanctification

> And it came to pass when the priests came out of the *Most* Holy *Place* (for all the priests

who *were* present had *sanctified themselves*, without keeping to their divisions. (2 Chronicles 5:11 NKJV, italics added)

Sanctification means being "set apart" for God and separating from toxic people and things. It means you set yourself apart to become more of an instrument God can use. Under Solomon's leadership, the priest sanctified themselves.

Consecrated priests sanctify themselves. That takes discipline. It takes a decision to commit to a process to be disciplined. Ultimately, if you want God to embody you and commit to you as an instrument he can use, you must commit to spiritual discipline. Before Solomon and Israel came to the point of revelation, they went through a period of sanctification. After that period of sanctification, God used them more powerfully.

Similarly, Jacob had to go through a process. He wrestled with God. Abram had to go through a process to become Abraham, and Saul was converted to Paul. Saul was a great persecutor of the Church and witnessed Stephen being stoned. However, his encounter with Jesus on the road to Damascus changed his life so much that he could say with revelation, "I am Paul." Sanctification is a scaling of the old man so God can reveal who you really are and use you for his purpose.

> *Sanctification is a scaling of the old man so God can reveal who you really are and use you for his purpose.*

The end result of the priests' sanctification was that the glory of God filled the Temple, and the priests could not stand to minister because of the glory.

> Indeed it came to pass, when the trumpeters and singers *were* as one, to make one sound to be heard in praising and thanking the LORD, and when they lifted up their voice with the trumpets and cymbals and instruments of music, and praised the LORD, *saying:* "*For He is* good, For His mercy *endures* forever," that the house, the house of the LORD, was filled with a cloud, **14** so that the priests could not [continue ministering because of the cloud; for the glory of the LORD filled the house of God. (1 Chronicles 5:13-14 NKJV)

Like the priests, Solomon's sanctification process is one of the things that caused God to respond the way he does in 2 Chron 7:14. The next in Solomon's process was communication.

Communication

> Yet regard the prayer of Your servant and his supplication, O LORD my God, and listen to the cry and the prayer which Your servant is praying before You: [20] that Your eyes may be open toward this temple day and night, toward the place where *You* said *You would* put Your name, that You may hear the prayer which Your servant makes toward this place. [21] And may You hear the supplications of Your servant and of Your people Israel, when they pray toward this place. Hear from heaven Your dwelling place, and when You hear, forgive. [22] "If anyone sins against his neighbor, and is forced to take an oath, and comes *and* takes an oath before Your altar in this temple, [23] then hear from heaven, and act, and judge Your servants, bringing retribution on the wicked by bringing his way on his own head, and justifying the righteous by giving him according to his righteousness. [24] "Or if Your people Israel are defeated before an enemy because they have sinned against You, and return and confess Your

name, and pray and make supplication before You in this temple, **25** then hear from heaven and forgive the sin of Your people Israel, and bring them back to the land which You gave to them and their fathers. **26** "When the heavens are shut up and there is no rain because they have sinned against You, when they pray toward this place and confess Your name, and turn from their sin because You afflict them, **27** then hear *in* heaven, and forgive the sin of Your servants, Your people Israel, that You may teach them the good way in which they should walk; and send rain on Your land which You have given to Your people as an inheritance. (2 Chronicles 6:19-27 NKJV)

At its most basic level, prayer is communication with God. In the passage from 2 Chronicles 6, Solomon kneels to pray with his hands lifted, and prays a prayer to dedicate the Temple. Are you in constant communication with God? As individuals and a nation, we must learn to constantly communicate with God.

There are three elements to his prayer to highlight. They are:

1. Solomon' Reverence
2. Solomon's Repentance

3. Solomon's Request

Solomon's Reverence

> . . . knelt down on his knees before all the assembly of Israel, and spread out his hands toward heaven); **14** and he said: "LORD God of Israel, *there is* no God in heaven or on earth like You, who keep *Your* covenant and mercy with Your servants who walk before You with all their hearts. (2 Chronicles 6:13b-14 NKJV)

Solomons' Repentance

> "But will God indeed dwell with men on the earth? Behold, heaven and the heaven of heavens cannot contain You. How much less this [c]temple which I have built! **21** And may You hear the supplications of Your servant and of Your people Israel, when they pray toward this place. Hear from heaven Your dwelling place, and when You hear, forgive. (2 Chronicles 6:18, 21 NKJV)

Solomon's Request

> Yet regard the prayer of Your servant and his supplication, O LORD my God, and listen to the cry and the prayer which Your servant is praying before You: **20** that Your eyes may be open toward this temple day and night,

> toward the place where *You* said *You would* put Your name, that You may hear the prayer which Your servant makes toward this place. (2 Chronicles 6:19-20 NKJV)

The posture of Solomon's heart speaks to humility. Humility means quiet reverence or to be modest or meek. We will unpack humility in more details as a part of the blueprint towards restoration in Chapter Three.

In Solomon's case, what else could cause God to respond to him with such power, depth, and promise in 2 Chronicles chapter seven? God's response has to do with Solomon's posture and the way he prayed—the posture of prayer.

Sometimes we think that prayer has to do with loudness and how we pray. Where there's prayer, there's power, and everyone prays differently. We don't know how Solomon prayed (what style), but we know it got results. Prayers that get results are prayers grounded in humility. They are prayed from a posture of humility. Jesus gives us a perfect example in Luke 18:

> Also He spoke this parable to some who trusted in themselves that they were

righteous, and despised others: **10** "Two men went up to the temple to pray, one a Pharisee and the other a tax collector. **11** The Pharisee stood and prayed thus with himself, 'God, I thank You that I am not like other men—extortioners, unjust, adulterers, or even as this tax collector. **12** I fast twice a week; I give tithes of all that I possess.' **13** And the tax collector, standing afar off, would not so much as raise his eyes to heaven, but beat his breast, saying, 'God, be merciful to me a sinner!' **14** I tell you, this man went down to his house justified rather than the other; for everyone who exalts himself will be [a]humbled, and he who humbles himself will be exalted." (Luke 18:9-14 NKJV)

Humility is not weakness or allowing people to walk over you. It is an attitude that respects and recognizes the presence of greater authority and honors that authority with modest speech and behavior.

Humility is not weakness or allowing people to walk over you. It is an attitude that respects and

> *recognizes the presence of greater
> authority and honors that authority
> with modest speech and behavior.*

It's not being afraid or feeling less than others, but it is responding and honoring the authority of another and knowing when to acquiesce and pay respect. Humility respects boundaries.

Solomon respected God's power, presence, and authority (and the history of who God had been in his father's life). He prays with a sense of honor and respect, and that posture causes God to respond in 2 Chronicles chapter seven. Do we pray with a posture of humility? Do we pray from a sense of honor and respect? Or do we pray with a tone that tells God what he should do? For example, "God, you better!" Even our decreeing and declaring should be done from a posture of honor and submission.

As a result of recognizing God's authority, Solomon receives revelation from God. And maybe some of us are not seeing the visitation of God because the posture of our hearts is not right. As James says, we pray amiss, from a selfish slant (I want my Mercedes, bills paid, etc.) versus praying for the intervention of God for the greater good. When he knows our heart is for the greater good, he'll bless us with the resources we need to bring transformation because he knows we're not just trying to build our personal kingdom. Remember, when visited by God, Solomon asked for wisdom, not riches. God responds by giving him the wealth of the world.

The three elements, Solomon's reverence, repentance, and request, cause God to respond with 'the blueprint' (the revelation) in 2 Chronicle chapter seven. We must examine our posture if we want a revelation from God.

Revelation

The revelation was God's response to a man that prayed in a way that pleased God. The revelation didn't just show up. We can pray because our backs are against the wall, and it's popular to pray, but are we really going to commit to building a foundation, sanctification, and communication. Those three steps are the blueprint to getting a blueprint—a revelation.

What is a revelation? Revelation means to reveal, pull back, and unearth. Revelation doesn't mean that whatever was revealed wasn't already there; something was blocking the person's sight. Revelation removes the barrier or blockage so the person can see what was there already.

For example, I once heard a story of some Tibetan monks who were charged with moving a clay statue in a monastery. However, it was so weighty they couldn't move it. One monk got curious to inspect it. One monk became so curious that one evening he took a hammer and chisel and slowly removed the clay debris from the statue. As he chiseled, he discovered that the clay statue wasn't clay. It was pure gold! During an enemy invasion of their land, monks in the monastery worked frantically to preserve many of their treasures by covering them with clay. In this way, their enemies wouldn't seize them because they would perceive that they were invaluable. The monk's chiseling away revealed something of great value.

If we want God to reveal what's value in us, we must allow him to 'chisel away' at the clay with which we've been covered.

Do you need a revelation from God? Do you need something that's covered up to be unearthed? God wants you to know there is something valuable in you, but you must undergo a 'chiseling' process. Once that process is complete, it provides direction for your life. You arise with a certainty—a soundness of who you are and your purpose.

Revelation provides direction. A revelation provides cooperation with God and others because it eliminates confusion.

In response to Solomon building a foundation, sanctification, and communication, God responds with 2 Chronicles 7:14 and gives a blueprint for national restoration. 2 Chronicles chapter seven is God's response to this process that Solomon went through. We should realize that Solomon models (demonstrates) critical elements of the formula (blueprint) before he receives it. A model is someone who demonstrates. People use models to show off clothes, model cars, etc. We need models in the world right now.

Solomon provides us a model—a framework, mold, prototype, first-generation example—or blueprint if you will—for how things should be in 2 Chronicles chapter six, which causes God to respond in chapter seven. God certifies and stamps the blueprint in his response. As a result of that model, Solomon gets revelation from God, which we will unpack in the next chapter as "the blueprint."

Chapter 3

Healing the Land: A Blueprint to Spiritual Restoration

There are two things panic patients hate to do. They hate to take medication—and they hate to go to the doctor. They hate to come to grips. — Earl Campbell

The best doctors and medicine in the world can't save you if you don't do what you're supposed to do. — Magic Johnson

Doctors commonly ask new patients for family health history, past individual ailments, and current medications. In addition, they ask patients to describe their symptoms and explain what's going on and the reason for their visit. Based on the patient's description and explanation, they order bloodwork and additional tests if needed.

Once a doctor reviews a patient's bloodwork and any additional test, they can provide a diagnosis. For some of us, hearing the news that we have cancer, diabetes, or another terminal illness would be devastating. But to embrace wellness, you also must embrace the illness! You must conclude that you are sick. Some people live in denial, however I have yet to see denial as a cure for an illness.

Then, the doctor can pinpoint the steps to remedy the situation and provide a diagnosis and prescription. That prescription is a framework, roadmap, and blueprint for the patient's wellness. Still, the patient must cooperate with the process and follow the given blueprint if they want to be well.

Like new patients, we all have symptoms called sins. However, following the doctor's prescription—the blueprint for wellness—to cure our sin ailment is necessary. We must follow the *Great Physician's* blueprint to see restoration, revival, and reconciliation in our world.

To begin, we must lay down our pride and humble ourselves. This is the first aspect of the blueprint that God gave Solomon in response to his prayers and concern for his nation. God told Solomon, "If my people, who belong to me, *humble themselves*, pray, seek to please me, and repudiate their sinful practices, then I will respond from heaven, forgive their sin, and heal their land" (2 Chronicles 7:14 NET, italics added). Inherent is God's response to Solomon's prayer was the blueprint (the prescription, the antidote) for revival, reconciliation, and restoration. However, there must be an acknowledgement that his people have a problem. Accordingly, we must first determine whether we have the disease named *humility deficiency*™.

Do we have humility deficiency™?

Humility deficiency™ is a spiritual condition when a person's pride, plans, and priorities take precedence over God's presence! It is pronounced by an "It's all about me, myself, and I" attitude and disposition toward life and others. It results in a warped perception of self and others that prevents an individual or nation from addressing its blind spots, demonstrating compassion, and walking in a right relationship with God as the Creator.

There are several examples of humility deficiency™. Let's first examine one from the book of James.

> Where do wars and fights come from among you? Do they not come from your desires for pleasure that war in your members? [2] You

lust and do not have. You murder and covet and cannot obtain. You fight and war. Yet you do not have because you do not ask. ³ You ask and do not receive, because you ask amiss, that you may spend it on your pleasures. ⁶ But He gives more grace. Therefore, He says: "God resists the proud, But gives grace to the humble." ⁷ Therefore submit to God. Resist the devil and he will flee from you. ⁸ Draw near to God and He will draw near to you. Cleanse your hands, you sinners; and purify your hearts, you double-minded. ⁹ Lament and mourn and weep! Let your laughter be turned to mourning and your joy to gloom. ¹⁰ Humble yourselves in the sight of the Lord, and He will lift you up. (James 4:1-3, 6-10 NKJV)

James is clear that wars and fights come from humility deficiency™—the warring of our desires and passions against the obvious choice for the good of others and God's agenda. He points out that the presence of Humility Deficiency™ is present at both national and individual levels. Many nations ask God to favor them in wars where there will be murder, destruction, and devastation. Similarly, on an individual level, James pushes back by saying that praying for that kind of outcome while possessing

Humility Deficiency™ will not bring God's favor! Why? Because you pride, plans, and priorities take precedence over God's presence!

However, James also presents the answer. He tells us that God gives grace to the humble. We should submit to God, resist evil, draw near to God, cleanse our hands, purify our hearts, and cry out in weeping for the state of our nation and what's going on in us and around us. Finally, James concludes, "humble yourself in the sight of God, and he will lift you up." James' pattern is much like 2 Chronicles 7:14. We cannot ignore it. There is an imperative to humble ourselves—for us to willingly come down from our high places and realize that no nation, land, or individual can experience healing without first humbling themselves.

Our next example of humility deficiency™ is Adam and Eve.

> Now the serpent was shrewder than any of the wild animals that the LORD God had made. He said to the woman, "Is it really true that God said, 'You must not eat from any tree of the orchard'?" **2** The woman said to the serpent, "We may eat of the fruit from the trees of the orchard; **3** but concerning the fruit of the tree that is in the middle of the

orchard God said, 'You must not eat from it, and you must not touch it, or else you will die.'" **4** The serpent said to the woman, "Surely you will not die, **5** for God knows that when you eat from it your eyes will open and you will be like God, knowing good and evil." **6** When the woman saw that the tree produced fruit that was good for food, was attractive to the eye, and was desirable for making one wise, she took some of its fruit and ate it. She also gave some of it to her husband who was with her, and he ate it. **7** Then the eyes of both of them opened, and they knew they were naked; so they sewed fig leaves together and made coverings for themselves. Now the serpent was shrewder than any of the wild animals that the Lord God had made. He said to the woman, "Is it really true that God said, 'You must not eat from any tree of the orchard'?" **2** The woman said to the serpent, "We may eat of the fruit from the trees of the orchard; **3** but concerning the fruit of the tree that is in the middle of the orchard God said, 'You must not eat from it, and you must not touch it, or else you will die.'" **4** The serpent said to the woman, "Surely you will not die, ⁵ for God knows that when you eat from it your eyes will open and you will be like God, knowing good and evil." ⁶ When the woman saw that the tree produced fruit that was good for food, was attractive to the eye, and was desirable for making one wise, she took some of its fruit and ate it. She also gave some of it to her husband who was with her, and he ate it. ⁷ Then the eyes of both of them opened, and they knew they were naked; so they sewed fig leaves together and made coverings for themselves. (Genesis 3:1-7 NET)

Eve allowed the serpent to entice her. That enticement introduced the Humility Deficiency to Eve. Eve had a choice. Do I prioritize God's presence or my pride? The bible says when Eve saw that the fruit was desirable and would make her wise, she acquiesced and ate the fruit—and unfortunately, Adam ate as well. Both lost their position and power with God because they thought the 'grass was greener on the other side. One of the things people must reconcile is that when you allow Humility Deficiency™ to rule, it's like a cancer that grows in the body. And if gone unchecked, it metastasizes, infecting other parts of the body.

Similarly, while God was orchestrating the Great Exodus of his people from Egypt, Pharoah demonstrated great pride and desire for exaltation. Clearly, God's desire was that his people would leave Egypt so they could worship him. He tells Moses to tell Pharoah to let his people go at least eight times in Scripture.

1. Afterward Moses and Aaron went in and told Pharaoh, "Thus says the Lord God of Israel: 'Let My people go, that they may hold a feast to Me in the wilderness.' " (Exodus 5:1 NKJV)

2. So Moses and Aaron went in to Pharaoh, and they did so, just as the Lord commanded. And Aaron cast down his rod before Pharaoh and before his servants, and it became a serpent. [11] But Pharaoh also called the wise men and the [b]sorcerers; so the magicians of Egypt, they also did in like manner with their [c]enchantments. [12] For every man threw down his rod, and they became serpents. But Aaron's rod swallowed up their rods. [13] And Pharaoh's heart grew hard, and he did not heed them, as the Lord had said. (Exodus 7:10-13 NKJV)

3. Go to Pharaoh in the morning, when he goes out to the water, and you shall stand by the river's bank to meet him; and the rod which was turned to a serpent you shall take in your hand. **16** And you shall say to him, 'The LORD God of the Hebrews has sent me to you, saying, "Let My people go, that they may serve Me in the wilderness"; but indeed, until now you would not hear! **17** Thus says the LORD: "By this you shall know that I *am* the LORD. Behold, I will strike the waters which *are* in the river with the rod that *is* in my hand, and they shall be turned to blood. **18** And the fish that *are* in the river shall die, the river shall stink, and the Egyptians will loathe to drink the water of the river." ' " **19** Then the LORD spoke to Moses, "Say to Aaron, 'Take your rod and stretch out your hand over the waters of Egypt, over their streams, over their rivers, over their ponds, and over all their pools of water, that they may become blood. And there shall be blood throughout all the land of Egypt, both in *buckets of* wood and *pitchers of* stone.' " **20** And Moses and Aaron did so, just as the LORD commanded. So he lifted up the rod and struck the waters that *were* in the river,

in the sight of Pharaoh and in the sight of his servants. And all the waters that *were* in the river were turned to blood. (Exodus 7:15-20 NKJV)

4. And the LORD spoke to Moses, "Go to Pharaoh and say to him, 'Thus says the LORD: "Let My people go, that they may serve Me. (Exodus 8:1 NKJV)

5. And the LORD said to Moses, "Rise early in the morning and stand before Pharaoh as he comes out to the water. Then say to him, 'Thus says the LORD: "Let My people go, that they may serve Me. (Exodus 8:20 NKJV)

6. Then the LORD said to Moses, "Go in to Pharaoh and tell him, 'Thus says the LORD God of the Hebrews:
"Let My people go, that they may serve Me. (Exodus 9:1 NKJV)

7. Then the LORD said to Moses, "Rise early in the morning and stand before Pharaoh, and say to him, 'Thus says the LORD God of the Hebrews: "Let My people go, that they may serve Me. (Exodus 9:13 NKJV)

8. So Moses and Aaron came in to Pharaoh and said to him, "Thus says the LORD God of the Hebrews: 'How long will you refuse to humble yourself before

Me? Let My people go, that they may serve Me. (Exodus 10:3 NKJV)

God spoke his will and desire for his people through his servant, Moses, so many times. Yet Pharaoh did not want to lose his labor force, status, and prestige among the nations. His hardness of heart and pride brought great demise to his nation. He had humility deficiency™.

Likewise, Nabal was a man of great wealth, flocks, sheepherders, and sheepshearers. David's army had dwelt among his herdsmen and shearers without him knowing. One day, in return for the protection David and his army had rendered, he asked Nabal for food for his troops. Nabal, whose name means fool, foolishly responded to the king with rudeness, pride, and insults. His wise wife, Abigail, had to step in.

> Now one of the young men told Abigail, Nabal's wife, saying, "Look, David sent messengers from the wilderness to greet our master; and he reviled them. **15** But the men *were* very good to us, and we were not hurt, nor did we miss anything as long as we accompanied them, when we were in the fields. **16** They were a wall to us both by night and day, all the time we were with them keeping the sheep. **17** Now therefore, know

and consider what you will do, for harm is determined against our master and against all his household. For he *is*
such a scoundrel that *one* cannot speak to him." **18** Then Abigail made haste and took two hundred *loaves* of bread, two skins of wine, five sheep already dressed, five seahs of roasted *grain,* one hundred clusters of raisins, and two hundred cakes of figs, and loaded *them* on donkeys. **19** And she said to her servants, "Go on before me; see, I am coming after you." But she did not tell her husband Nabal. **20** So it was, *as* she rode on the donkey, that she went down under cover of the hill; and there were David and his men, coming down toward her, and she met them. **21** Now David had said, "Surely in vain I have protected all that this *fellow* has in the wilderness, so that nothing was missed of all that *belongs* to him. And he has repaid me evil for good. **22** May God do so, and more also, to the enemies of David, if I leave one male of all who *belong* to him by morning light." **23** Now when Abigail saw David, she dismounted quickly from the donkey, fell on her face before David, and bowed down to the ground. **24** So she fell at his feet and said: "On me, my lord, *on* me *let* this
iniquity *be!* And please let your maidservant speak in your ears, and hear the words of your maidservant. **25** Please, let not

my lord regard this scoundrel Nabal. For as his name *is,* so *is* he: Nabal *is* his name, and folly *is* with him! But I, your maidservant, did not see the young men of my lord whom you sent. **26** Now therefore, my lord, *as* the LORD lives and *as* your soul lives, since the LORD has held you back from coming to bloodshed and from avenging yourself with your own hand, now then, let your enemies and those who seek harm for my lord be as Nabal. **27** And now this present which your maidservant has brought to my lord, let it be given to the young men who follow my lord. **28** Please forgive the trespass of your maidservant. For the LORD will certainly make for my lord an enduring house, because my lord fights the battles of the LORD, and evil is not found in you throughout your days. **29** Yet a man has risen to pursue you and seek your life, but the life of my lord shall be bound in the bundle of the living with the LORD your God; and the lives of your enemies He shall sling out, *as from* the pocket of a sling. **30** And it shall come to pass, when the LORD has done for my lord according to all the good that He has spoken concerning you, and has appointed you ruler over Israel, **31** that this will be no grief to you, nor offense of heart to my lord, either that you have shed blood without cause, or that my lord has avenged himself. But when the LORD has dealt well with my lord, then remember your maidservant." **32** Then David said to Abigail: "Blessed *is* the LORD God of Israel, who sent you this day to meet me! **33** And blessed *is* your advice and blessed *are* you, because you have kept me this day from coming to bloodshed and from avenging myself with my own hand. **34** For indeed, *as* the LORD God of Israel lives, who has kept me back from hurting you, unless you had hurried and come to meet me, surely by morning light no males would have been left to Nabal!" **35** So David received from her hand what she had brought him, and said to her, "Go up in peace to your house. See, I have heeded your voice and respected your person." **36** Now Abigail went to Nabal, and there he was, holding a feast in his house, like the feast of a king. And Nabal's heart *was* merry within him, for he *was* very drunk; therefore she told him nothing, little or much, until morning light. **37** So it was, in the morning, when the wine had gone from Nabal, and his wife had told him these things, that his heart died within him, and he became *like* a stone. **38** Then it happened, *after* about ten days, that the LORD struck Nabal, and he died. **39** So when David heard that Nabal was dead, he said, "Blessed *be* the LORD, who has pleaded the cause of my reproach from the hand of

> Nabal, and has kept His servant from evil! For the LORD has returned the wickedness of Nabal on his own head." And David sent and proposed to Abigail, to take her as his wife. **40** When the servants of David had come to Abigail at Carmel, they spoke to her saying, "David sent us to you, to ask you to become his wife." **41** Then she arose, bowed her face to the earth, and said, "Here is your maidservant, a servant to wash the feet of the servants of my lord." **42** So Abigail rose in haste and rode on a donkey, attended by five of her maidens; and she followed the messengers of David, and became his wife. (1 Samuel 25:14-42 NKJV)

Nabal's Humility Deficiency™ brought calamity and judgement upon his life. Fortunately for him, Abigail had the presence of mind to appease David's wrath through repentance and humility. All these examples help us see that God hates pride but exalts the humble. He expresses is disgust for pride in Proverbs.

> These six things the Lord hates, Yes, seven are an abomination to Him: [17] A proud look, A lying tongue, Hands that shed innocent blood, [18] A heart that devises wicked plans, Feet that are swift in running to evil, [19] A false witness who speaks lies, And one

who sows discord among brethren. (Proverbs 6:16-19 KJV)

For too long be we have thumbed our nose at God and desecrated his commands and laws as if our ways are better. Could it be that the same outcome Nabal, Adam, and Eve suffered are a result of our Humility Deficiency™? Isaiah reminds us, "For my thoughts are not your thoughts, neither are your ways my ways" (Isaiah 55:8-9 KJV).

Curing Humility Deficiency™

Like so many physical ailments, the cure to the humility deficiency™ necessitates the active involvement of the patient. The one suffering from humility deficiency™ must voluntarily, humble themselves. Remember James' instruction:

> But He gives more grace. Therefore, He says: "God resists the proud, But gives grace to the humble." [7] Therefore submit to God. Resist the devil and he will flee from you. [8] Draw near to God and He will draw near to you. Cleanse your hands, you sinners; and purify your hearts, you double-minded. [9] Lament and mourn and weep! Let your laughter be turned to mourning and your joy to gloom. [10] Humble yourselves

in the sight of the Lord, and He will lift you up. (James 4:1-3, 6-10 NKJV)

He reveals the steps to humbling yourself, including:

1. Submit to God.
2. Resist the devil.
3. Draw near to God.
4. Cleanse your hands.
5. Purify our hearts.
6. Cry out to God in weeping for the state of our lives and nation.

This is God's prescription to cure humility deficiency™. Perhaps the reason we're not seeing the exaltation, revival, breakthrough, and healing is because of humility deficiency™?

Like a patient who goes to a doctor, we must follow the blueprint God prescribes for healing our land.

The Blueprint

If my people, who belong to me, humble themselves, pray, seek to please me, and repudiate their sinful practices, then I will respond from heaven, forgive their sin, and heal their land. (2 Chronicles 7:14 NET)

This is the blueprint God revealed to Solomon in 2 Chronicles 7. It was in response to his prayers and humility in 2 Chronicles 6. The first element of the blueprint is humbling ourselves, for which there are many benefits. We have seen the pitfalls from the lives of Adam, Eve, Pharoah, and Nabal. Let's look at the benefits from humbling ourselves as revealed through the life of Moses.

Humble Ourselves

Miriam and Aaron were speaking against Moses for marrying and Ethiopian woman. In response to their gossip and undermining of towards Moses leadership, God brings wrath upon them, striking Miriam with leprosy, causing her to be shut of the camp of Israel for seven days. While the judgment that came upon Miriam and Aaron was rightful, so is what God what reveals about Moses' humility. People who walk in humility receive affirmation. The Bible says in Numbers, "Now the man Moses was very meek [humble], above all the men which were upon the face of the earth" (Numbers 12:3 KJV).

As a result of the outward opposition from Miriam and Aaron, God spoke up for Moses, affirming his character that he was his chosen leader. Walking in humility will not guarantee you won't have opposition, but it does provide the security of knowing that when people oppose you, God's got your back!

People who walk in humility receive access.

> The Lord said of Moses, ". . . Hear now my words: If there be a prophet among you, I the LORD will make myself known unto him in a vision and will speak unto him in a dream. My servant Moses is not so, who is faithful in all mine house. With him will I speak mouth to mouth, even apparently, and not in dark speeches; and the similitude of the LORD shall he behold: wherefore then were ye not afraid to speak against my servant Moses?" (Numbers 12:6-8 KJV)

In other words, Moses' humility earned him access that no one else received—invitations others crave and favor many would die for! Miriam and Aaron's arrogant, pompous, undermining, loud-mouthed, and critical disposition towards Moses severed their relationship with God! May I challenge you? Do you need a miracle? Walk in humility! Do you need access? Walk in humility! Do you need an answer from God? Walk in humility! This is the first step in the blueprint. The next step is equally as vital—prayer.

Corporate Pray: Communicating With God

God positioned Solomon as king. People who are in leadership are often looked upon to guide, direct, and inspire. Solomon did this when he prayed before the people corporately. His corporate prayer of dedication pleased God so much that God made it a condition that if there was ever a departure from his commands one of the ways that his creation could get back in alignment with him was through prayer, and more specifically, corporate prayer. So, when God responds to Solomon about healing the land, he is calling his people not only to individual prayer but also corporate prayer.

What is corporate prayer? It is when a group of individuals collectively call on God with a humble heart. In Scripture, God calls on his creation to corporately call on him with different types of prayers, including prayers of reverence and petition. Prayers of reverence are prayers of worship, honor, and celebration. Prayers of petitions are prayers that include a request, either personal petition or corporate supplication for God to do something on our behalf, the behalf of his Church, or our nation(s). There is power in agreement when we come together in corporate prayer, and this is a vital aspect of healing our land.

Seek His Face: Pursuit

If we want to see restoration, revival, and reconciliation in our world, we must consistently pursue the presence of God. Pursuit involves action. Like many of the action movies where someone is taken hostage and a hero must actively pursue the perpetrators to get the person back, we must actively pursue God's presence.

For example, in the movie Taken with Liam Neeson, Neeson's daughter is taken by human traffickers who, had intensions on selling her on a secret underground black market. The moment his daughter was taken, Neeson is relentless in eliminating her capturers and returning his daughter home safely.

When God tells Solomon to 'seek his face' it is in the spirit of that same understanding. After we've humbled ourselves and prayed, God desires for us to exhibit an insatiable appetite to constantly seek to know more of him. David said in Psalm 42, "As the deer pants for the water so my soul longeth after thee." When an animal is thirsty, it will trek for miles and miles, using its sense of taste and smell to locate water—to quench its thirst.

We must never become content in our present knowledge or pursuit of God. Why? Because the more we pursue him, the more of himself he reveals. Consider Moses. As he pursued God, God used him to perform ten miraculous acts against Egypt which freed Israel. God used him to part the Red Sea, feed Israel with manna from heaven, bring water from a rock, and gave them the Ten Commandments. His consistent pursuit of God opened opportunities for him to know God at a greater level.

Turn From Our Wicked Ways

During the past twenty years, there's been a shift away from traditional paper maps to GPS systems. Year ago, when you went on a trip, you'd call AAA to draw out a map of the directions to your destination. Now, with an increasing number of satellites in the sky, technology has not made it possible for us to get to our destination safer, faster, and with less confusion. A unique feature of most GPS systems is the ability for it to "talk" to the driver or dictate the directions. It tells you when to go left, when to go right, and when to keep straight. More advanced systems alert you of stop lights, construction zones, and even potential weather hazards. However, the most unique feature is it alerts you when you've past a turn, or completely gone in the wrong direction. When that occurs, the GPS will say, "Make a U-Turn." Other times it will say, "When it's safe, make a U-Turn."

In God's response to Solomon's prayer, he outlines the final step in the blueprint to appease his wrath and release blessing over his people—turn from your wicked ways. The word turn in the Hebrew context means a complete and total separation. It is a departure and to divorce. It is a complete reversal from something. It's a "U-Turn."

God clearly outlined to Solomon that if his people make a complete departure from their evil ways, he will heal the land. Evils ways in the sight of God were always associated with divided worship—divided loyalty. According to Exodus 20, in the Ten Commandments, God told Moses to tell the people, "Thou shalt have no other gods before me—for the Lord thy God is a Jealous God." God clearly wanted all the focus and attention of his people. Therefore, in the event that they allowed their attention to be diverted, if they wanted God's blessing and approval, there needed to be a departure from what God deemed evil. They had to separate from evil and focus on what God deemed as good and godly.

As a world, we must understand that God is clearly speaking from heaven, saying, "Make a U-turn!" Repent! Turn from your wicked ways! Even though there is rampant evil in our land, the good news is, God wants to heal our land.

What was a healing land then? A nation or land God that was healed is one that is free from political distress: no outcry in the streets; social distress: a morally upright populace, especially the young men and women; and economic distress: economic and agricultural abundance.[2]

What would constitute a healed land now? A world where the people are completely and totally surrendered to the will and purpose of God. And completely dedicated to following his Word as he gives us grace. Is it a tall feat? Absolutely! Is it possible? Yes! So how we do it? Follow Jesus' model of the Blueprint.

Jesus modeled the Spiritual Blueprint, consistently humbling himself, praying, seeking God's face, and turning away from sin. No wonder everywhere Jesus

---

[2] Olubi Johnson, "Turning from Our Wicked Ways," SPCC Online, accessed March 5, 2023, https://www.spcconline.org/present-truth/turning-from-our-wicked-ways

went, he could heal the sick, raise, the dead, open blinded eyes, and unstop deaf ears. He was completely committed to the blueprint. And as a result, God could trust him as an instrument of praise for his glory and honor.

The question is how much of an instrument for God do you want to be? What kind of instrument do we want to be for God? One that just exists or one that is in prime shape. God is trying to create a grand piano, but you must buy into what it will take to become that grand piano. For example, my Grandma's China closet was not for everyday use—maybe Sunday, Christmas, and Thanksgiving. It was preserved for something special and what God is trying to create in you is not everyday or regular. Sometimes, God will put you in a special place and get you prepared to be used at a special time. You can't look at your walk as just a paper plate. You'll never be highly used of God like fine China.

God wants us to come to the place of being in prime condition for him to use us. For example, as a musician, I could play a piano or organ that was broken down, missing keys, out of tune, and in disrepair. I'd make a modest sound—and perhaps impress many people with my ability to adapt to the instrument's failed state. But I commit to repairing the instrument: fixing the legs so it can stand correctly, and fixing the keys so I don't miss a note. I must schedule to have it tuned regularly. Then when

I go to perform, the sound I make truly brings 'music to the ears' of my listeners!

When we humble ourselves, pray, seek his face, and turn from our wicked ways, what we are saying to God is, "I want to be primed and ready to be an instrument for you." Jesus committed himself to that discipline. So should we.

Let's follow the blueprint to bring healing to our land.

About the Author

Pastor Stephen E. Boyd, author, speaker, church-planter, musician, producer, and singer-songwriter, is a rising influential leader whose impact is gaining national and international attention. Affectionately known as the 'Professor of Praise' his life's mission is to help ordinary people experience the power of an extraordinary God! To book Pastor Boyd to speak, sing, coach, or consult, or to find out more about the ministry, please contact Terrell Sarver at: 803-570-2675, or email terrellsarver@gmail.com. You may also visit Pastor Boyd's website at: www.iamstephenboyd.com and his social media pages:

Facebook:
@iamstephenboyd
@iamstephenboydmusic

IG:
@iamstephenboyd
@iamstephenboydmusic

www.ingramcontent.com/pod-product-compliance
Lightning Source LLC
Chambersburg PA
CBHW061732040426
42453CB00026B/982